one would come after me, he must deny himself an

★ ★ ★

FOLLOWER
LIVING AN AUTHENTIC FAITH

★ ★ ★ This Book Belongs To

★ ★ ★ Date

Powered by: LeaderTreks

Follower: Living An Authentic Faith, Follow Up Journal
Copyright © 2013 by youth**ministry**360. All rights reserved.

Published by **LeaderTreks** in the United States of America.

ISBN 13: 978-1-935832-29-4
ISBN 10: 1935832298

Author: Andy Blanks
Design: Upper Air Creative

Then Jesus said
to his disciples,
"If anyone would
come after me, he
must deny himself
and take up his cross
and **follow me**."
—Matthew 16:24

CONTENTS

Getting Started   1

WEEK 1

Week 1 Intro   3
Day 1   5
Day 2   7
Day 3   9
Day 4   11
Day 5   13
Day 6   15
Day 7   16
Looking Ahead   18

WEEK 2

Week 2 Intro   21
Day 1   23
Day 2   25
Day 3   27
Day 4   29
Day 5   31
Day 6   33
Day 7   34
Looking Ahead   36

WEEK 3

Week 3 Intro   39
Day 1   41
Day 2   43
Day 3   45
Day 4   47
Day 5   49
Day 6   51
Day 7   52
Looking Ahead   54

WEEK 4

Week 4 Intro   57
Day 1   59
Day 2   61
Day 3   63
Day 4   65
Day 5   67
Day 6   69
Day 7   70
Follower Wrapping Up   73

Getting Started . . .

SO HERE YOU ARE . . .

You're holding an interactive journal that will serve as your guide for an in-depth look at what it means to be a FOLLOWER. This means at some point in the not-so-distant past you probably spent some time going through the *Follower* study with your youth group.*

Maybe you thought you were done talking about the concept of following. Maybe you thought you had learned all there was to learn.

The truth? You're just getting started.

You see, there is a lot to consider when we think of our lives as followers, so much that we could never have covered it all in a four session study at a weekend event or retreat. So, you're about to get the opportunity to go even deeper into this look at what it means to truly live an authentic faith.

So, embrace it. Give it your best. Commit to sticking with this book until the end. It will only take a few minutes each day.

You'll be happy you did.

LET'S GET STARTED. LOOK AT THE NEXT PAGE TO LEARN HOW THIS BOOK WORKS.

*You definitely don't have to have gone through the FOLLOWER study with your group to get a ton out of this journal. But, it might help some to have already been introduced to it.

Here are a few things you need to know to put this book to good use.

START WITH THIS ADVICE
Whether you're super-committed and read your Bible each day or struggle to read a few verses a couple of times a week, the key to sticking with this through four weeks is a routine. Try and work through this book at the same time each day, whether that's in the morning, after lunch, or before you go to bed. Block out a time each day to spend in this book, and then commit to sticking to it. **You'll find it's a lot easier to stay consistent that way.**

HAVE YOUR BIBLE OPEN
Resist the urge to ignore the spots where this book will tell you to read a passage of Scripture. This book is only a guide for *the* Book. **The close relationship with God that you want only happens by reading and doing what's in the Bible.** Have it open as you go through this book.

EACH WEEK IS STRUCTURED THE SAME, BUT IS REALLY DIFFERENT
Each week's content works in similar ways. **But, each day is different. And, there are a lot of different kinds of activities.** Some will take 3-5 minutes, some 10-15. Some will ask you to look at two or three passages of Scripture; some will just ask you to think about a concept. The variety will make it easier to stick with and help you learn in different ways that are suited to you.

WHAT IF I MISS A DAY OF READING? OR THREE?
Don't give up! Take this at your pace! The goal is for you to grow closer to God and to have a faith-life that's more "real"! If you miss a day or two . . . or four . . . don't throw in the towel. Pick this book back up and start where you left off. **You can do this!** And by doing it, you'll show the world that God makes an incredible difference in the lives of His followers. So, hang in there! You've got this!

Well, that's what you need to know to get started! **Turn the page to read the introduction to Week 1.**

WEEK 1 INTRO

Before starting Week 1, read this short introduction

Chances are you have this book in your hands because sometime in the recent past you spent some time with your youth group studying through *Follower*. Maybe it was a few days ago. Maybe it was a few weeks ago. Either way, it's a safe bet that you're reading this because you want to learn more about what it means to follow God.

Good for you. The pursuit of a more authentic faith is a sign that you're really searching for God. That's awesome. The Bible says God comes close to us when we come close to Him. Take God up on this promise. Expect to see Him more as you become more of a follower.

Even if you just wrapped up your time with your group in *Follower*, we're going to take this first week and take one more look at the concepts you studied with your group. Why? Because life happens. You're busy. And your mind and heart have probably been distracted some since you last thought about these concepts. Take this first week to remind yourself what you learned.

And if you didn't already go through the study of *Follower* with a group, then here's your chance to get a fresh start.

So, let's get started! Turn to page 5 for Week 1, Day 1.

Read the passages below and follow the prompts to interact with them on page 6.

The idea behind *Follower* is to ask one question: What does it look like to live out an authentic faith? While this question is fleshed out in depth throughout Scripture, we can look to Jesus' first words to His disciples and learn a lot about the foundation of a faith that's real.

Read these following passages:

From that time on Jesus began to preach, "Repent, for the kingdom of heaven is near."18 As Jesus was walking beside the Sea of Galilee, he saw two brothers, Simon called Peter and his brother Andrew. They were casting a net into the lake, for they were fishermen. 19 "Come, follow me," Jesus said, "and I will make you fishers of men." 20 At once they left their nets and followed him. 21 Going on from there, he saw two other brothers, James son of Zebedee and his brother John. They were in a boat with their father Zebedee, preparing their nets. Jesus called them, 22 and immediately they left the boat and their father and followed him. — Matthew 4:17-22

As Jesus went on from there, he saw a man named Matthew sitting at the tax collector's booth. "Follow me," he told him, and Matthew got up and followed him.—Matthew 9:9

The next day Jesus decided to leave for Galilee. Finding Philip, he said to him, "Follow me."—John 1:43

NOW, TAKE A MOMENT AND ANSWER THE FOLLOWING QUESTIONS:

1. What does it take to be a Christian?

If you answered "faith," or "belief," you're correct. We are saved from the penalty of our sins through faith in Jesus' words and work. The Bible says that when we believe that Jesus is who He said He was, namely the Son of God come to take away our sins, we're saved by the grace of God. Got it? Now, next question.

2. What impact should your faith have on your life? In other words, in what ways should your faith in God change you? Think in terms of big picture stuff as well as day-to-day, practical things.

Our faith should change our lives. The Bible says in 2 Corinthians that when we come to believe in Jesus, we're transformed into new creations. Our old sinful selves die. In their place is a new, transformed life.

3. Look at what Jesus called the disciples to in those verses on page 5. What did He ask them to do?

Following Jesus is the foundation of living an authentic faith. Following Jesus means not following you. It is belief in action. It's a faith that says, "Jesus, my life will not be all it can be unless I faithfully let you set my course." We'll be talking more about this, but for now think about this:

4. What comes to mind when you think of when you think about following someone?

Stay tuned for tomorrow's devotion on Page 7 and 8. You're going to love it.

How did Jesus define what it meant to follow Him? Let's take a closer look.

First, read Matthew 16:24 then answer the questions that follow:

> 24 Then Jesus said to his disciples, "If anyone would come after me, he must deny himself and take up his cross and follow me.—Matthew 16:24

• Underline the places where Jesus defines what it means to follow Him.

• What areas in your life are the hardest to surrender to Jesus?

• Why do you think Jesus told us that in order to follow Him we have to deny our own plan and leadership of our life's direction?

Next, read John 12:25-26. Then answer the question below.

> 25 The man who loves his life will lose it, while the man who hates his life in this world will keep it for eternal life. 26 Whoever serves me must follow me; and where I am, my servant also will be. My Father will honor the one who serves me.—John 12:25-26

In the space provided, think of one place where Jesus is calling you to join Him. This can be a group of people, a neighborhood in your city, even a team or club. Where does Jesus want you to go join Him as He works?

WHAT WILL IT TAKE FOR YOU TO GO JOIN HIM?

Finally, read Matthew 10:37-39 and answer the following prompts.

> [37] "Anyone who loves his father or mother more than me is not worthy of me; anyone who loves his son or daughter more than me is not worthy of me; [38] and anyone who does not take his cross and follow me is not worthy of me. [39] Whoever finds his life will lose it, and whoever loses his life for my sake will find it."—Matthew 10:37

Let's remember that Jesus isn't saying there's anything wrong with loving our families. He's making a point by using an extreme example. He's saying that we're supposed to be so dedicated to loving and following Him, that it's wrong when something as good as our love for our families gets in the way.

List three things that sometimes come in the way of your dedication to following God.

1.

2.

3.

Which one of these is the easiest to address?

What will it take to put Christ above this particular thing?

Which one of these is the hardest to change?

Write a short prayer to God asking Him to show you how to fix this priority problem, and to give you the strength to let nothing come between you and your commitment to follow Him.

Take the chance today to spend some time thinking about your relationship with God. Let the following verse guide you.

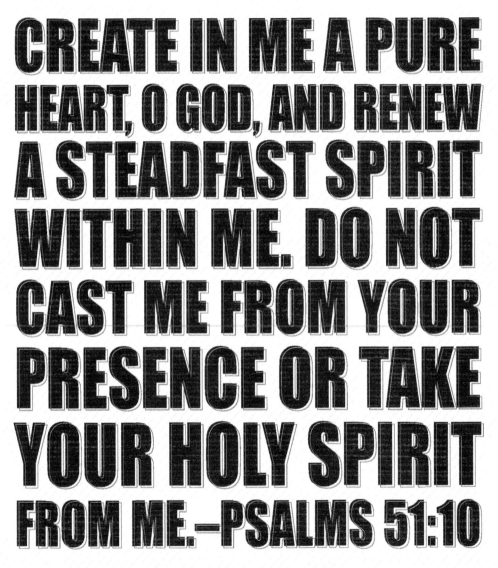

CREATE IN ME A PURE HEART, O GOD, AND RENEW A STEADFAST SPIRIT WITHIN ME. DO NOT CAST ME FROM YOUR PRESENCE OR TAKE YOUR HOLY SPIRIT FROM ME.—PSALMS 51:10

TAKE SOME TIME TODAY TO PRAY TO GOD. ASK HIM TO
CLEANSE YOUR HEART SO THAT YOU SEE NOTHING BUT HIM.
LISTEN TO WHAT HE SAYS TO YOU. LOOK AROUND YOUR
WORLD FOR HOW HE MIGHT SPEAK TO YOU TODAY.

The Bible provides direction and encouragement for us as we follow Christ. Look at the phrases below and choose one that has a message you need right now. Then, follow the arrow from the phrase to the box on page 12. Follow the instructions there.

BE INTENTIONAL ON YOUR JOURNEY
1 Corinthians 9:24-27

BE STRONG WHEN IT GETS TOUGH
2 Corinthians 4:7-9

BE ENCOURAGED THAT THE SPIRIT GOES WITH YOU
John 14:25-27

BE MOTIVATED BY CHRIST
Hebrews 12:1-3

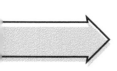

YOUR JOURNEY WITH GOD TAKES FOCUS AND INTENTIONALITY. PRAY TODAY AND ASK GOD TO REMIND YOU TO FOCUS ON HIM.

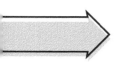

LIFE IS HARD. BUT GOD GOES WITH YOU. PRAY AND ASK GOD TO REMIND YOU TODAY OF HIS PRESENCE.

YOU AREN'T ON THIS JOURNEY ALONE. PRAY AND THANK GOD FOR SENDING HIS SPIRIT TO BE WITH YOU.

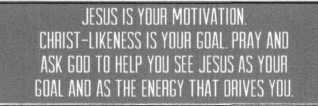

JESUS IS YOUR MOTIVATION. CHRIST-LIKENESS IS YOUR GOAL. PRAY AND ASK GOD TO HELP YOU SEE JESUS AS YOUR GOAL AND AS THE ENERGY THAT DRIVES YOU.

Read today's devotional and spend some time journaling. Seriously, even if you don't love to write, you'll be surprised how helpful it is.

You're first week of focusing on what it means to be a follower is almost over.

Take a moment and journal some thoughts. Yeah, yeah, yeah . . . you don't like to journal. Here's the deal: You don't have to write a novel, just a few thoughts. The goal is to both think about your thoughts (something you probably don't do a ton of considering how fast paced your life is), and to have them down on paper so you can look back on them.

So, see all that blank space over there on page 14? Put some words in that space.

Think About This . . .
- How do you feel about your current life as a follower? How is it going? Are you happy with where you are (of course, knowing you will always be growing closer to Christ)? Or do you know you're not where you'd like to be?
- How important is your faith to you right now? Are you willing to do what it takes to get it back on track?
- Where is God leading you? What are you passionate about? How could God use you to pursue your passion in His name?

WEEK 1: DAY 6

Read this and reflect on it through the day.

Hopefully this week you learned something about what it means to live out your faith.

Living out your faith means following God, not anyone else. Being a Christian is so much less about what you say or don't say, wear or don't wear, where you go or don't go, and what you listen or don't listen to.

Being a Christian is not about us vs. them. It's not just about being a rule follower or a "good" person. And it's not as simple as just believing.

Now let's be clear on something: salvation is a belief thing. You believe and you're saved. End of story. But here's the deal: the Bible never separates salvation from life change. When the Bible talks about belief, it's a belief that motivates action.
Your new life is proof of your saving faith. And a life of action-fueled faith looks a lot like following Jesus.

Following Christ is what it looks like to live as a new creation.

Will you accept the challenge to daily follow Jesus?

Take today off...
YOU'VE EARNED IT.

★ ★ ★

But let your mind dwell on the things you've been learning. Listen to God. Think about what your life would be like if you followed Him so closely you wouldn't even have to think about where He was leading you . . . you'd just know. That can be a reality for you, you know. Let that sink in today.

LOOKING AHEAD . . .

HERE'S A PREVIEW OF WHAT'S COMING UP NEXT WEEK:

Week 2: Day 1—Bible Study: Matthew 7:13-14
Week 2: Day 2—A *Following* Fact
Week 2: Day 3—A Picture of A Follower
Week 2: Day 4—A *Follower* Quote
Week 2: Day 5—Following With Others: Friends On Your Journey

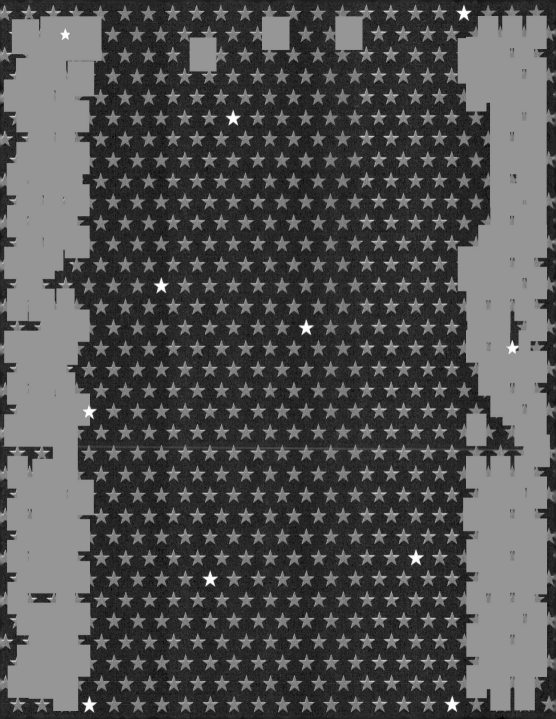

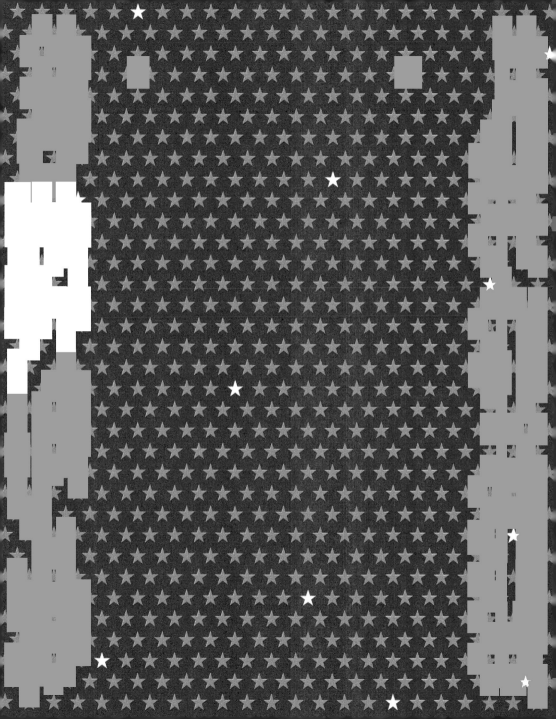

WEEK 2 INTRO

Living an authentic faith isn't done in a vacuum. It's lived out in the real world, with real pressures, temptations, and challenges.

It's also not lived out alone.

Your faith journey constantly intersects with others. Your life impacts and affects people all the time. And your life is in turn impacted and affected by others as well.

What impact do the pressures of the world have on you? How do other people change how you follow, both for the positive and the negative? How can you make a big difference in the lives of those you meet while following Jesus?

You'll get a chance to answer these questions and more this week.

What are you waiting for?

WEEK 2: DAY 1

Read the following devotion and answer the questions on page 24.

> "Football wasn't designed to be easy. If it was easy, everybody would want to play it. Football teaches sacrifice. And sacrifice teaches excellence." – Pat Dye, Football Coach, Auburn University, 1981-1992

What Coach Dye said about football is true about many things in life, isn't it? You could say it about relationships, another sport, learning a musical instrument or another skill, and so on. The easy way is often the wrong way. Most things in life worth having are worth working hard to obtain.

Is it wrong to think of our faith that way? Is it wrong to think about following Jesus as something that is hard, but rewarding? Let's see what Jesus said about it.

Take a moment and read Matthew 7:13-14. This passage comes in the middle of Jesus' Sermon on the Mount. This is where Jesus was teaching His disciples, and others, the ways of God's Kingdom and how children of God are to live and interact in the world. Most of Jesus' teachings would have surprised His audience, as they were contrary to much of the popular understanding of the day.

What is Jesus saying here? He is saying that it is much easier to go with the crowd on the wide, easy-to-navigate roads. The gate is wide and easy to pass through. But it leads to eternal separation from God. The gate that leads to life in Christ? It's narrow. Not everyone will pass through it. Why? The road is hard. It's tricky. It requires bravery, and sacrifice, and most of all, faith.

Following Jesus isn't easy. Jesus knew that. But kind of like that quote at the top of the page, Jesus knew that the sacrifice itself would lead to greater trust in Him and a more fruitful life for us.

TAKE A FEW MOMENTS AND THINK ABOUT YOUR ANSWERS TO THE FOLLOWING QUESTIONS. WRITE DOWN YOUR ANSWERS IF YOU CHOOSE.

1. How does your faith and trust in God help lead you along the narrow road?

2. When is it the hardest for you to stay true to following God?

3. When you work to submit your will to God in the tough times, letting Him lead you by faith, how does it teach you more about God? How does it teach you more about you?

4. Have you ever thought to thank God for the hard times? For the times when you have to rely on Him even more because things are tough? Now might be a good time for that. Thank God for seeing you through the rough patches on the road of following after Him.

There are certain basic truths about following Christ. Here's one of them.

FOLLOWING FACT:

YOU WERE CREATED TO FOLLOW JESUS. BUT YOU WEREN'T CREATED TO FOLLOW JESUS ALONE. **GOD GIVES YOU FRIENDS** TO SUPPORT AND ENCOURAGE **YOU ON YOUR JOURNEY.**

Here's a little something the Apostle Paul said in his letter to the Christ-followers in Rome:

> "May the God who gives endurance and encouragement give
> you a spirit of unity among yourselves as you follow Christ Jesus."
> —Romans 15:5

Paul knew what it was like to follow Jesus. Paul followed Jesus in some of the darkest places imaginable. He was beaten, ridiculed, and ran out of town. He also followed Jesus through some amazingly bright moments. Through most of it, Paul had companions with him. He had friends who walked with him on this journey. He shared the lows and the highs with others.

Notice that Paul links the ideas of endurance and encouragement with the idea of being unified among friends.

Having other followers to follow with you on your journey gives you energy, encouragement, and confidence to keep going.

THINK ABOUT THIS . . .

• Who is your closest friend that is also a Christ-follower?

• How important is your faith in your relationship?

• Do you encourage each other in your journey with Christ? If not, why not?

The Bible gives us a lot of examples of people who committed to follow Jesus.
Here's one. (You'll find another on page 63.)

★ A PICTURE OF A FOLLOWER ★

THE FOLLOWER WHO WAS FORGIVEN

If we're not careful we can forget that the Christ-followers in the Bible weren't perfect. They goofed up just like us, which can actually make it a little easier to relate to them. Their example helps us understand that we can follow Jesus in spite of our flaws.

One of these folks was a guy named John Mark. If you've read the Gospel of Mark, you've partaken in his handiwork. But there was a time when John Mark dropped the ball. It cost him, but in the end he was forgiven and restored. Here's the story . . .

Mark, who most people think was Barnabas' cousin, went with the Apostle Paul and Barnabas on their first missionary journey. While we don't know all the details, somewhere along the way, Mark bailed out. Based on what we can gather from Scripture, it seems to have happened when the going got tough.

Paul got pretty frustrated about this, to the point of actually getting into a disagreement with Barnabas over Barnabas' insistence on bringing Mark on their second journey. The disagreement was such that they actually agreed to split up and part ways.

It sure looks like Mark screwed up pretty badly. But, that's not the end of the story.

Somewhere along the way, Mark was forgiven and restored by Paul. How do we know? Here's what Paul says about Mark years later in Paul's letter to Timothy:

> "Get Mark and bring him with you, because he is helpful to me in my ministry."—2 Timothy 4:11

How's that for forgiveness? Mark went from being on Paul's naughty list to being essential to his ministry. While we don't know the details, we can connect the dots. We know Paul showed grace to Mark. And we know Mark must have learned from his mistakes and matured in his faith. (And we can guess that this continued: later Peter would write that Mark was like a son to him (1 Peter 5:13).)

Mark was a Christ-follower. Mark made mistakes. But Mark picked himself up and kept going. This is encouraging for us.

When we blow it, it doesn't mean we're out of the game. God gives us grace. And like Paul redeemed Mark, God redeems us, using us as we grow closer to Him.

Today is a little more relaxed. Read the following quote and follow the prompts on the next page.

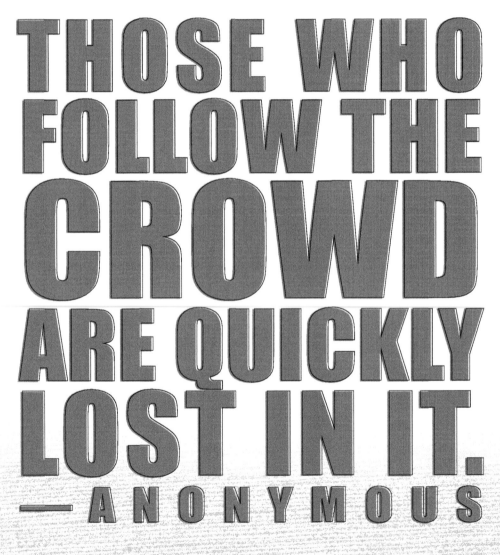

THOSE WHO FOLLOW THE CROWD ARE QUICKLY LOST IN IT.
— ANONYMOUS

SPEND SOME TIME REFLECTING ABOUT THIS QUOTE. RECORD YOUR THOUGHTS IN A JOURNAL, ON THE PAGE BELOW, OR ON A NOTE TAKING APP. THINK ABOUT THEM AS YOU GO THROUGH THE DAY TODAY AND TOMORROW.

- Why is it easy sometimes to go follow the crowd?

- Why is it hard sometimes to follow Jesus?

- When you follow the crowd you can get lost. What are the results of following Jesus?

WEEK 2: DAY 5

Read the following devotion. *Then follow the instructions on page 32.*

The Bible makes it clear: we are called to do life together as we follow God. Scripture has a ton of places where this is fleshed out in a variety of ways. Need proof? Here are just a few places where we see this at work:

> Calling the Twelve to him, he sent them out two by two and gave them authority over evil spirits.—Mark 6:7

> After this the Lord appointed seventy-two others and sent them two by two ahead of him to every town and place where he was about to go. He told them, "The harvest is plentiful, but the workers are few. Ask the Lord of the harvest, therefore, to send out workers into his harvest field.—Luke 10:1-2

> I long to see you so that I may impart to you some spiritual gift to make you strong—that is, that you and I may be mutually encouraged by each other's faith.—Romans 1:11-12

> Carry each other's burdens, and in this way you will fulfill the law of Christ.—Galatians 6:2

> Join with others in following my example, brothers, and take note of those who live according to the pattern we gave you. —Philippians 3:17

> For where two or three come together in my name, there am I with them.—Matthew 18:20

> As iron sharpens iron, so one man sharpens another.—Proverbs 27:17

See . . . told you this idea was all over the Bible.

Follow the prompts below to apply the truth of these verses in your life.

FIRST, TAKE A MOMENT TO THINK OF THE TWO OR THREE CLOSEST FRIENDS WHO YOU WOULD
SAY ARE FOLLOWING GOD IN THEIR LIVES.

NEXT, LOOK AT THE VERSES ON PAGE 31. CHOOSE A VERSE THAT REMINDS YOU OF THESE FRIENDS,
OR THAT ENCOURAGES YOU TO LEAN ON YOUR FRIENDS AS YOU EACH FOLLOW CHRIST, OR THAT
CHALLENGES YOU. WRITE THE VERSE BELOW.

THEN, TAKE A MOMENT AND PRAY FOR THESE FRIENDS. PRAY THAT GOD WOULD DRAW YOU
CLOSER TOGETHER AS EACH OF YOU STRIVE TO LIVE AN AUTHENTIC FAITH.

FINALLY, TAKE A MOMENT AND TEXT AT LEAST ONE OF THEM AND TELL THEM YOU PRAYED FOR
THEM. TELL THEM THANKS FOR BEING A GOOD FRIEND.

You weren't meant to follow God alone. Good thing He's given you friends to
travel with you on your journey.

WEEK 2: DAY 6

Read this and reflect on it through the day.

Your journey to follow God is your own.

No one else can live it for you.

But you're not alone in your journey. You have people walking alongside you as you collectively follow God. And your path will ultimately intersect with others on their own journeys, some of them toward God, some of them in the opposite direction.

Your life has tremendous potential to impact others, both for the positive and for the negative. How you will use it is up to you.

The only thing that's a given is that you can't have zero influence. You can't pass through this world and have zero impact. Every time you bring glory to God it's a positive impact. And every time you fail to do that, whether it's because you did something harmful or did nothing at all, you make a negative impact.

So, be bold. Live life loud. Pursue God even when it's hard . . . especially when it's hard. Join with others. Link up with solid friends who are like-minded. Bring new followers along. Make a difference.

Whatever you do, don't waste your chance to make a difference.

But don't stop thinking about God today. Don't stop listening to Him. Especially as He reminds you of those people who He's put in your life for a reason.

Look around you. Who is in your life who is committed to following Christ? Thank God for him or her today.

LOOKING AHEAD . . .
HERE'S A PREVIEW OF WHAT'S COMING UP NEXT WEEK:

Week 3: Day 1—Bible Study: Romans 12:1-2
Week 3: Day 2—Tools for the Journey
Week 3: Day 3—Following With Others: Guides
Week 3: Day 4—A Follower Fact
Week 3: Day 5—A Follower Quote

FOLLOWER

LIVING AN AUTHENTIC FAITH

★ ★ ★

... one would come after me, he must deny himself...

WEEK 3 INTRO

Here's a truth that's important to keep in mind:

To follow someone, you have to know where he or she is going.

You can't follow your friend to a new restaurant if you lose her in traffic, right?

The same principle applies to our ability to follow after Jesus. We can't follow Him if we don't know where He wants to take us. We don't know where He wants us to go if we don't know Him.

Knowing Jesus gives us incredible insight into where He might ask us to go in our journey. This week will focus on what that looks like, how it happens, and why it's important.

You may be ready to follow. But first, you have to know where you're headed.

Read the following devotion and answer the questions on page 42.

How do you know what God wants for your life? The Apostle Paul had some good advice for some other Christ-followers about 2,000 years ago.

Read Romans 12:1-2. If you remember, Romans is a letter Paul wrote to all of the Christ-followers in Rome. He wanted to come see them and encourage them in their newfound faith. Romans was Paul's way of giving them a really in-depth view into the study of God. Romans is an awesome Bible book as it contains a really thorough look at Paul's teachings on grace and Christ.

In Romans 12:1, Paul teaches the Romans that their lives are to be offered to God as "sacrifices." This is Paul's way of saying that their lives are to be given over to God to be used however He wills. By doing this, they are worshiping God. Verse 2 goes further, with Paul urging the Romans not to be like the world around them, but to strive to be like God.

Paul tells the Romans to do this by transforming their minds. For us, this can be taken as a call to know God, to learn about Christ through studying the Bible. When we come to Christ in faith, our lives are transformed. But the more we come to know Him, the more we will see the world as God does.

The coolest thing of all is that Paul says by doing this, we'll know God's will for our lives. By knowing God, we'll know what He wants for our lives. We'll know where He's headed, which makes it a lot easier to follow.

THINK ABOUT THE FOLLOWING QUESTIONS. IF YOU CHOOSE, WRITE YOUR ANSWERS DOWN IN THE SPACE PROVIDED.

1. How well do you know God? What steps are you taking in your life to know Him more?

2. Can you think of an example of how following the world's ways is different than following God's ways?

3. Do you ever think about what God wants from your life? How do you know where He is leading you?

4. How often are you aware of seeing the world around you through God's eyes? What does that mean to you? And what does it have to do with how close you are to God?

To follow God we have to know Him. There are a few definite ways we can know God.
Work through this activity to learn what you can do to know God more.

How do we get to know God? There are a few main ways we can learn about God and His ways.

The primary way we come to know God is to read the Bible. God gave us the Bible so that we could meet Him in the pages, learning all we need to know about Him in order to follow Him. Secondly, we can pray to God. Prayer is how we talk and listen to Him. Another way is to serve others. We come to know God more when we give of our time and energy helping others in His name. Finally, we can know God by looking for Him in His creation. Being aware of God in the world around us is a profound way of knowing Him.

Now look over at page 44. Each cylinder represents one of these four areas. For each cylinder, color in a portion of the cylinder to represent how you're doing in that area. If you're strong, you might color in the entire cylinder. If it's an area you could improve in, you might color in only half. Then, in the shade box below, write down some specific, practical things you can do in the coming days and weeks to grow in these areas.

REMEMBER, YOU CAN'T FOLLOW GOD IF YOU DON'T KNOW HIM. DO WHAT IT TAKES TO GET TO KNOW GOD MORE.

Read The Bible

Pray

Serve Others

See God In Nature

Who has helped guide you on your journey? *Work through the following activity to discover the importance of people helping you follow Jesus.*

> "But you, Timothy, man of God: Run for your life from all this. Pursue a righteous life—a life of wonder, faith, love, steadiness, courtesy. Run hard and fast in the faith. Seize the eternal life, the life you were called to, the life you so fervently embraced in the presence of so many witnesses."—1 Timothy 6:11-12 (The Message)

Read that passage you see above this. Did you know this comes from a letter written from Paul, an old man nearing the end of his life and ministry, to a young pastor named Timothy? Paul had taken Timothy under his wing years earlier, when Timothy was just a boy. Paul loved Timothy like a son, constantly encouraging him, teaching him, and modeling a life lived in devotion to God. Paul's influence helped shape Timothy into an able leader of the church.

Paul's example here is one we should look to. We were never intended to follow God on our own. We've talked about this truth already in this book. But in addition to friends who accompany us on our journey, we have guides as well.

Throughout our lives, we will have people who invest in us, shaping us, leading us to follow Christ as they are following Christ. These people are put in our lives by God to help us draw closer to Him.

Spend a moment on the next page thinking about the guides who have made a difference in your life.

Use this space to journal your thoughts. Not much of a journaler? Then simply read the prompts below and think about your responses.

1. Who has had the most influence on your life as a Christ-follower?

2. Have you taken the time to let this individual know of his or her impact on you? What do you think it would mean to them to hear it from you?

3. If you haven't had someone in your life who has guided you as you follow Jesus, is there someone you can reach out to who might meet that need for you?

4. You're called to be a guide to others as well. What's keeping you from leading others in their spiritual journeys?

There are certain basic truths about following Christ. Here's another one of them.

FOLLOWING FACT:

OTHER PEOPLE ARE WATCHING YOU AS YOU FOLLOW CHRIST. YOU'RE NOT PERFECT. BUT BE AWARE THAT THE WAY YOU LIVE OUT YOUR FAITH INFLUENCES OTHERS.

It might not always seem fair to you, but people are watching you. People at your school know you're a Christ-follower and they're looking to see how you live it out.

Are they watching to see if you fail? Some of them are, for sure.

But there are a lot of people you encounter who see something different about you. And they want what you have. Maybe they know Jesus already but they see in you a deeper faith. Don't shy away from this. The Apostle Paul didn't.

In his first letter to the Corinthian church, Paul wrote:

"Follow my example, as I follow the example of Christ."
—1Corinthians 11:1

Paul understood that he had an impact on the people around him, a Christ-centered impact. Other people are watching you as you follow Christ. Instead of seeing this as a burden, see it as an opportunity to be used by God to help others see Him.

Today is a lighter day. *Read the following quote and follow the prompts on the next page.*

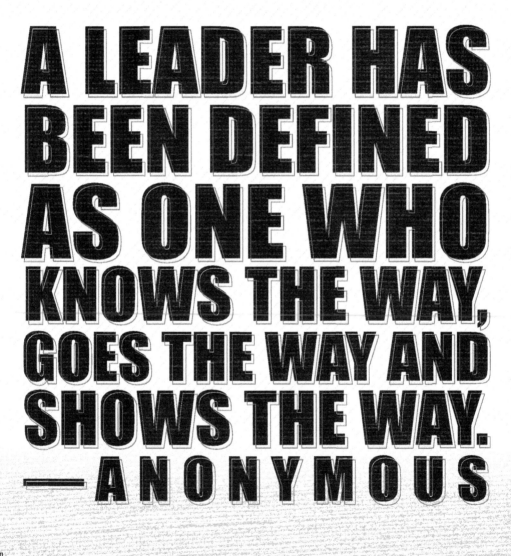

A LEADER HAS BEEN DEFINED AS ONE WHO KNOWS THE WAY, GOES THE WAY AND SHOWS THE WAY.
—ANONYMOUS

- How does this relate to yesterday's devotion?
- Why is it important to have someone in your life who knows the way and shows the way?
- What's wrong with knowing the way but not going the way?
- How close are you to meeting this definition of leadership? What's standing in your way?

WEEK 3: DAY 6

You're almost done with this study. Just one more week remaining.

One more week to be challenged each day to follow God. Were you challenged this week? Hopefully you understand how important it is to know God. As we've said many times before, you can't follow someone you don't know.

But to be sure, knowing God can't be motivated by anything other than love. You should want to know God simply because you want to know God. After all, this is the supreme creator of the universe we're talking about here. The Alpha and the Omega. The Author of Life.

When we realize that God has actually chosen to be made known to us, we should be immediately humbled by this fact. We should be motivated to know God because it's possible to know Him.

Make seeking God a priority on your life. If you don't truly know God, following Him becomes more about being trying to be "good" under your own power than about a relationship with your Savior.

God knows you. And He loves you. He wants you to know and love Him. What are you waiting for?

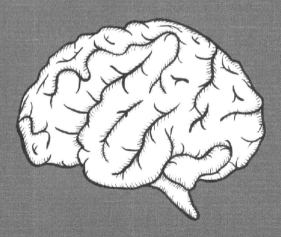

Enjoy a day off.
ENJOY IT, WE MEAN TRULY ENJOY IT.

★ ★ ★

Take some time today and really soak in the world around you. See God in His creation. Thank Him for it. And praise Him by having as much fun today as you possibly can.

LOOKING AHEAD . . .

HERE'S A PREVIEW OF WHAT'S COMING UP NEXT WEEK:

Week 2: Day 1—Hide the Word
Week 2: Day 2—A *Following* Fact
Week 2: Day 3—A Picture of A Follower
Week 2: Day 4—A *Follower* Quote
Week 2: Day 5—Who Are You Following?

WEEK 4 INTRO

And so you're getting ready to wrap up this final week in this journal.

Good for you for sticking with it. That's actually pretty awesome.

You know, most people can't stick with something like this book for four weeks. And that's kind of sad, right? Our attention spans aren't even long enough for us to give God a few minutes a day for a month.

But if you're the kind of person who is still engaged with this journal, you're probably the kind of person who takes his or her relationship with God pretty seriously.

You're probably the kind of person who strives to follow Jesus.

You're almost done with this book. Hang in there. This last week is a good one. You won't be disappointed. And hopefully, you'll be challenged one more time to live an authentic faith.

Ready? Let's finish strong . . .

WEEK 4: DAY 1

Do you know what it means to hide God's Word in your heart? Well, you're about to.

To be a follower, you have to know the way to go. God's character, as it's revealed in the Bible, is the truest map for life we have. That's why it's important to know God's Word. Have you ever memorized a verse before? It's a lot easier than it sounds.

One of the easiest ways to memorize Scripture is the 5-5-5 model. The idea is to choose a verse, then read the verses five times out loud (slowly). When you're done there, say the verses out loud five times without looking at your Bible. Finally, without looking, write the verses five times.

Once you do that, you've pretty much got them locked in.

It's important to hide God's Word in your heart because in the process of saying them over and over, you'll actually begin to internalize their truths. They'll be right on your heart and mind!

So, take this opportunity to learn the verse you see below. Practice the 5-5-5 method using page 60 to write your verses. Here's your verse:

> "Then Jesus said to his disciples, 'If anyone would come after **me**, he must deny himself and take up his **cross** and **follow me**.'" Matthew 16:24

Give it a try! You may just be surprised how fun it is to know God's Word inside and out. Dwelling on the Bible is one of the most powerful ways to grow as a Christ-follower.

There are certain basic truths about following Christ. Here's another one of them.

FOLLOWING FACT:

TO FOLLOW GOD YOU HAVE TO KNOW WHERE HE'S GOING. YOU HAVE TO "KEEP IN STEP" WITH HIM, LISTENING AND OBEYING THE HOLY SPIRIT'S LEADING.

It's impossible to follow someone if you don't know where he or she is headed. Like following a car in heavy traffic, you can get off track if you don't know where you're supposed to be going. The Apostle Paul gives us some advice on how to know where God is heading.

In his letter to the Christ-followers in the region of Galatia, Paul said this:

> "So I say, live by the Spirit, and you will not gratify the desires of the sinful nature . . . Since we live by the Spirit, let us keep in step with the Spirit."—Galatians 5:16 and 25

Living "by the Spirit" speaks to the focus of our lives, how we are to pursue godliness instead of worldliness. "Keeping in step" with the Spirit speaks to the day-to-day way we're supposed to live our lives. The Spirit leads us to live as Christ lived, and to see the world through God's eyes.

Paul knew that staying in tune with the Spirit's leading by seeking His guidance and listening to His voice is the only way to follow God. After all, following God is easier when we know exactly where He's headed.

WEEK 4: DAY 3

The Bible gives us a lot of examples of people who committed to follow Jesus. You've looked at one already. Here's another.

★ A PICTURE OF A FOLLOWER ★

THE HESITANT FOLLOWER

We can have the best intentions. We can want to follow Christ, but our sinful natures can keep us from doing so, or from doing so as effectively as we'd like.

Do you remember who Nicodemus was? He was a Pharisee, who were the dudes who were constantly after Jesus. He was also a member of a group called the Sanhedrin, which was kind of like a Jewish city council. In other words, Nicodemus was in the camp of folks against Jesus.

But Nicodemus saw something in Jesus that made his heart twitch a bit. He came to Jesus at night, so his friends wouldn't know that he approached Jesus, asking questions that showed his heart was hungry, if hesitant. (Read their encounter in John 3:1-21.) In response, Jesus gave him a ton of truth, holding nothing back.

Here's the deal, Nicodemus left his encounter with Jesus without giving us any hint of how he would respond. From the story in John's Gospel, we don't know if Jesus' words affected him.

Would he become a follower of Christ?

Here's the cool thing, while we can't be 100% sure, there are signs that Nicodemus did indeed become a Christ-follower. Later in the book of John, we see Nicodemus defend Jesus in front of a hostile group (John 7:50-52). And when Jesus was crucified and buried, who was it helping prepare the grave? You guessed it. Nicodemus was there (John 19:39-40).

So, Nicodemus might have been hesitant at first. But all the signs point to the fact that sometime along the way, he began a following relationship with Christ.

Think About This...
• When have you been hesitant to follow Christ in the past?
• What makes you hesitate to follow Christ today?
• How can you trust God to help you become more bold in following Him?

Today is a lighter day. *Read the following quote and follow the prompts on the next page.*

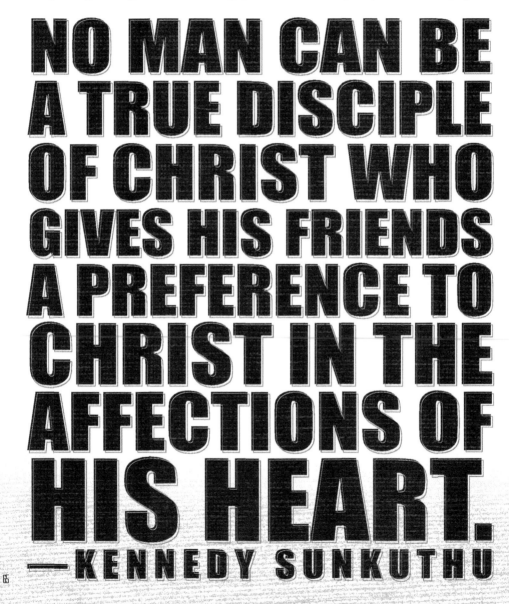

NO MAN CAN BE A TRUE DISCIPLE OF CHRIST WHO GIVES HIS FRIENDS A PREFERENCE TO CHRIST IN THE AFFECTIONS OF HIS HEART.

—KENNEDY SUNKUTHU

- How does this quote hit you? Is there any tension over who is most influential in your life?

- What are some examples of how you may give your friends a more important place than Jesus in terms of the decisions you make?

- What does it feel like to know that you are following closely after Christ?

WHO ARE YOU FOLLOWING?

We all follow someone. Who do you follow? Maybe you follow the world. You know, maybe you live your life trying to become the kind of people you see on TV, movies, and advertising. Maybe you chase trends and acceptance. Or maybe you follow yourself. Maybe you're an individual. Maybe you don't listen to anyone. Not God. Not others. Or maybe, just maybe, you follow a version of Jesus that you or someone else has tailor made to fit your own personal preferences. Maybe you follow a Jesus who doesn't ask much of you, a Jesus you only talk to when you need something, a Jesus that is contained. A Jesus that is safe. The problem is, none of these people are in any way suited to lead you. The world isn't. You aren't. And a Jesus you've twisted and shaped doesn't even exist, so He's not leading you anywhere. There is life to be found only in following the one true God, the only God fit to lead, the only God fit to follow. Follow Him. Do whatever you have to do to follow Him. Surrender it all. Set your focus on Him and go where He leads. You will never find real meaning, real purpose, or real happiness unless you do.

WE ALL FOLLOW SOMEONE.
WHO DO YOU FOLLOW?

Congratulations.

Seriously. You deserve it. You showed a lot of focus and discipline to finish this book.

Did you learn a lot about what it means to live out an authentic faith?

Is your understanding of God different? Do you have a new perspective for what it means to be His child? Hopefully you do.

Hopefully, you've gained a new perspective on what being a Christ-follower is all about. This is a perspective that is capable of launching your relationship with God into a new orbit. The knowledge you've learned over the past few weeks will open your eyes to a deeper walk with God.

Give yourself a little pat on the back for seeing it through.

As usual,
**THIS DAY
IS ON THE
LIGHTER SIDE.**

★ ★ ★

But, you have one task for today. Somewhere in the bottom part of this page, summarize what you've learned over the past four weeks in one sentence.

Think about this concept as you go through the next couple of days. Consider how it has impacted your understanding of faith.

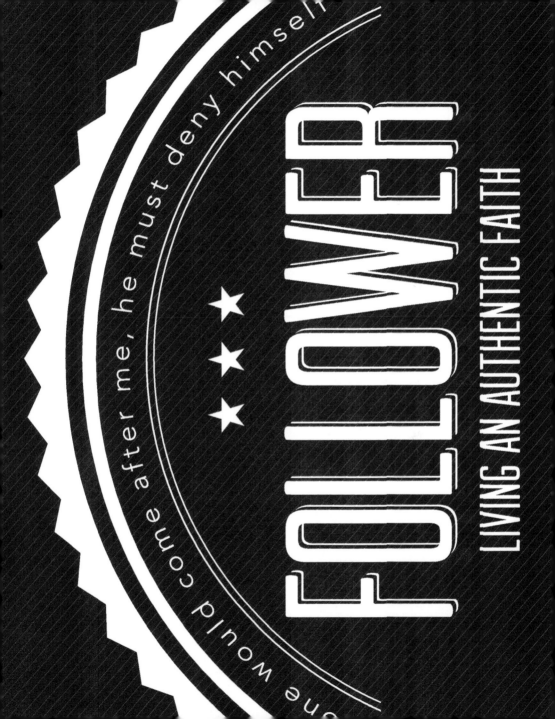

FOLLOWER WRAP UP

Your relationship with God is the most important aspect of your life.

IT MIGHT NOT ALWAYS SEEM THAT WAY, BUT IT'S TRUE.

Your life will be powerfully shaped by how you understand God, how well you know Him, how your knowledge of Him impacts your actions and thoughts. Your faith isn't just something you do. It's not a club you belong to. It's not a feeling. It's an all consuming part of your very existence.

And how you approach your faith will determine how your life is spent.

You have the potential to live a meaningful life full of purpose and possibility.

But you also have the potential to live a life of barely getting by, of choosing yourself over God. You have the potential to live a life un-moved by God.

Which is really no life at all.

So, what will it be?

What will you choose? A lukewarm faith? Or the authentic faith of a follower?

There are consequences for both. One choice may very well lead to, at worst, separation from God, and at best, a watered down faith that failed to impact you or the world.

On the other hand, choosing to follow God opens up amazing possibilities. It will broaden your worldview, your heart for others, and your grasp of God and His purpose for your life. There will be costs to choosing to follow Him. They are to be expected. But true followership is a reward unlike any other. One you'll never look back on.

Don't miss your chance to live a bold, authentic faith. Accept God's call to be a follower, not just a fan. Take a chance with God. Let Him show you what's waiting for you.

Commit yourself to living your life as a true follower of Christ. Once you start in this journey and get a real taste of life on mission with God, you'll never look back.

What are you waiting for?

ABOUT THE AUTHOR

Andy Blanks is the Co-founder and Publisher for youthministry360. Andy is passionate about God's Word and the transformation it brings in the lives of God's people. What brings Andy the greatest joy is seeing teenagers become sold-out disciples of Christ, following the Lord no matter the cost, and influencing the world around them in the name of Jesus. Andy is a writer, teacher, speaker, and a lifelong Boston Red Sox fan. He lives in Birmingham, AL with his wife, Brendt, and their three daughters and one son.

NOTES:
All quotations taken from *THE COMPLETE GATHERED GOLD, A treasury of quotations for Christians*. John Blanchard, ed. Evangelical Press, 2006.